All at Sea!

Pirate Pete

Sam Snorkel

"I'm Pirate Pete and these are my friends Millie, Dolly and Sam. Join us on our nautical adventure! Make my telescope and look out to sea. For a life on the ocean wave float your own boat with Sam. Dive beneath the surface with Dolly and meet a scary sea monster. Join Millie making undersea mosaics and finally arrive back at your very own beach!"

Millie the Mermaid

Dolly Diver

Make a telescope like Pirate Pete's!

Sailors used telescopes to see things a long way off: enemy ships, foreign ports and desert islands.

① Roll the large rectangle into a tube and fix into place.

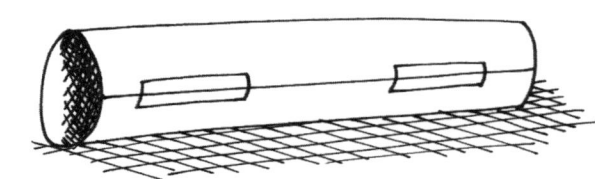

fix with sticky tape or glue

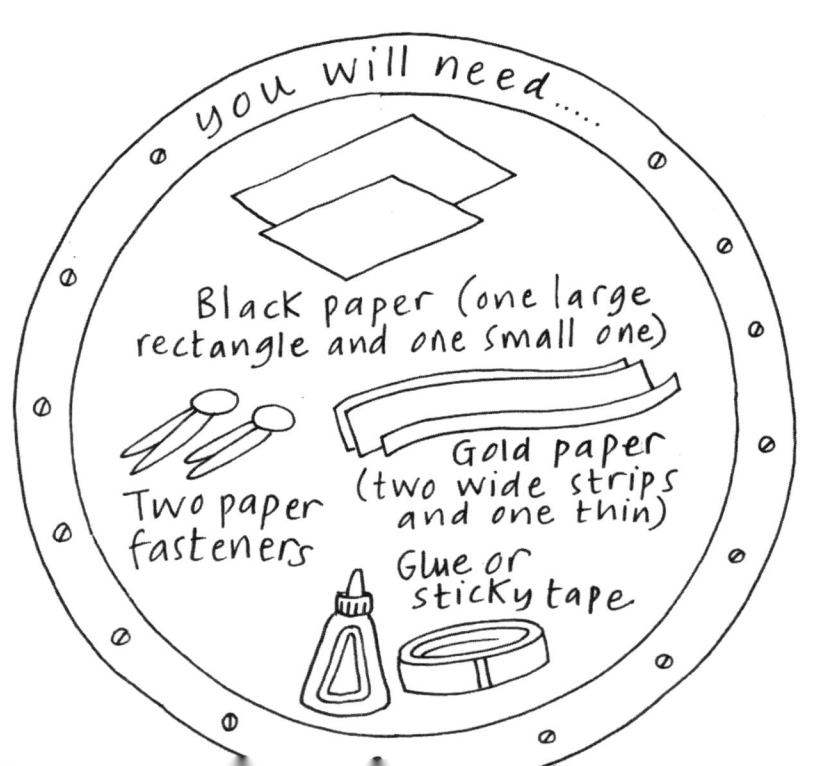

You will need....
- Black paper (one large rectangle and one small one)
- Two paper fasteners
- Gold paper (two wide strips and one thin)
- Glue or sticky tape

② Roll the smaller rectangle into a tube and stick into place in the same way.

③ Slide the smaller tube into the larger tube and secure it with the paper fasteners.

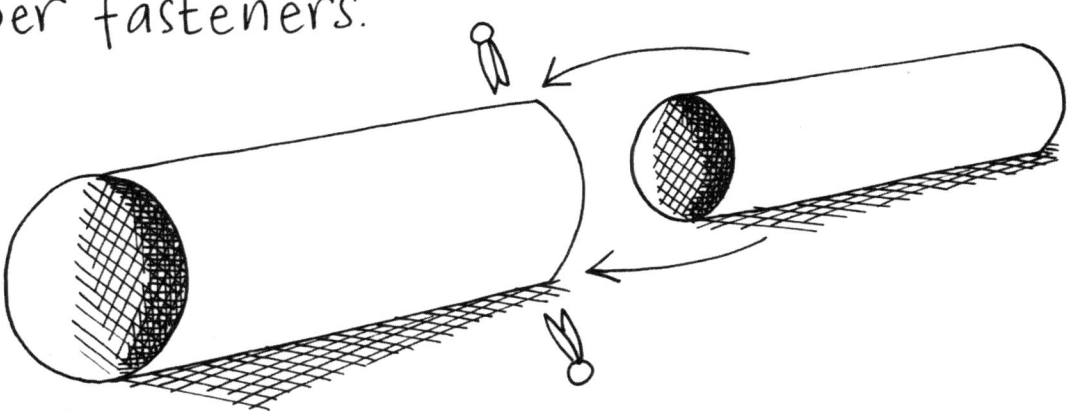

④ Finally wrap one thick strip of gold paper around each end of the larger tube. Then wrap the thin strip of gold paper around the end of the smaller tube. If you don't have any gold or black paper you could always use magazine pages and kitchen foil instead. If you don't have paper fasteners use sticky tape.

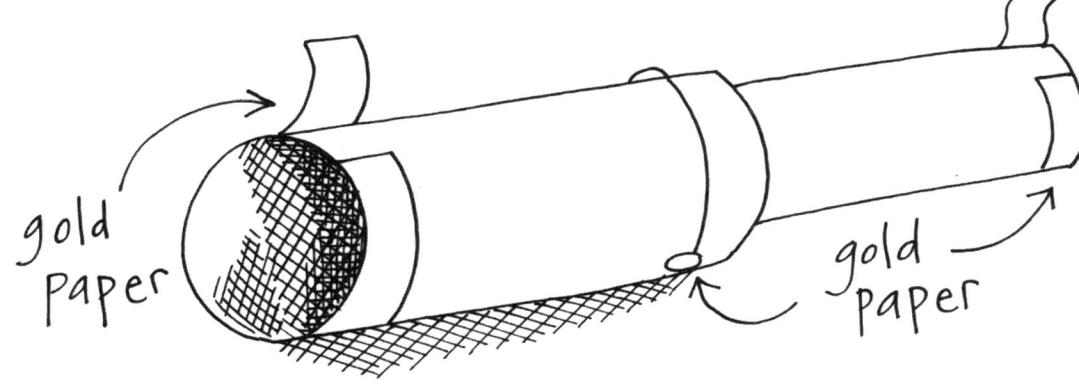

Sam Snorkel floats some boats!

(ask an adult to help you float the boats)

When you look out to sea or visit a busy port you will see many different kinds of boats... big ones, small ones, wooden ones and metal ones. When you get home you can make your own fleet!

Experiment with different sized paper for different sized boats and colour them as brightly as you can. You can even race them in a sink or bath but remember to turn off the taps — you might need an adult to help you!

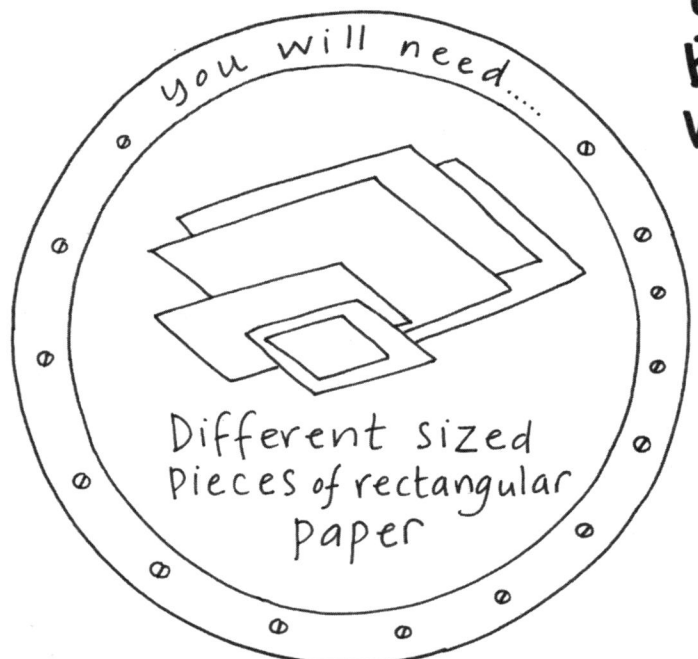

you will need....
Different sized pieces of rectangular paper

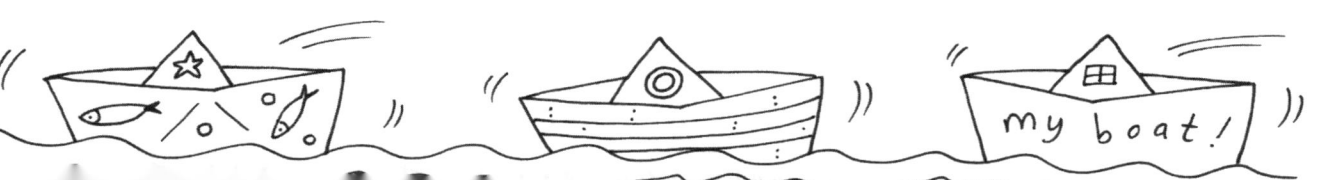

my boat!

Start your boat building here!

① Fold the paper in half.

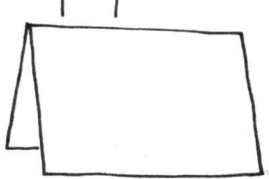

② Then fold in two of the corners. (nearest to the folded edge to make a point)

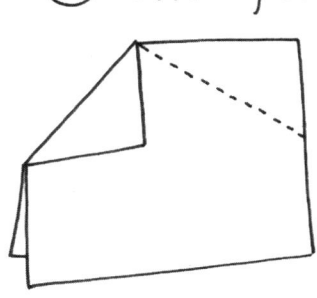

③ Fold up both the flat edges against the triangle on each side.

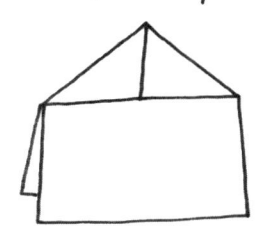

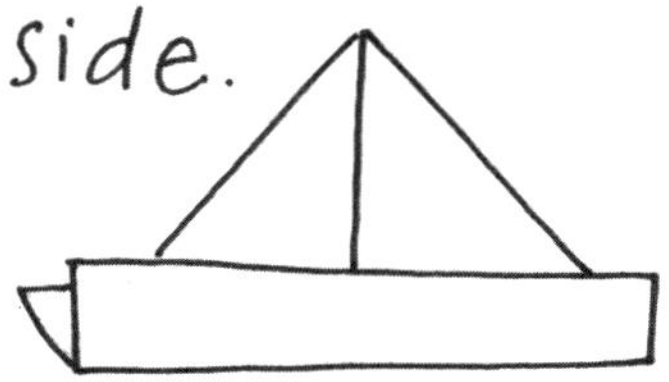

④ Then open it out as if it was a hat. (you can even try it on if no one's looking!) Press corner Ⓐ against corner Ⓑ and fold flat into a square.

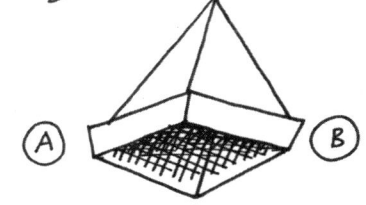

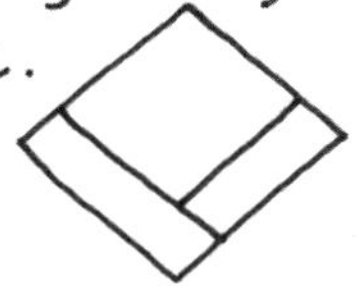

⑤ Tuck in the flap on each side and fold each side upward to make another triangle.

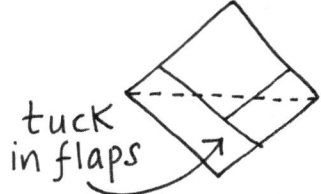

tuck in flaps → fold upwards

⑥ Open up this triangle as you did before and push corner Ⓐ to corner Ⓑ again.

⑦ Now pull the two halves apart and your boat will pop up!

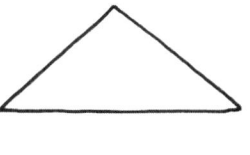

Why not decorate your boat with a fishy design!

Dolly meets a Scary Sea monster!

Dolly finds all sorts of strange things on her dives, but she has seen nothing stranger than the creatures that live at the bottom of the ocean.

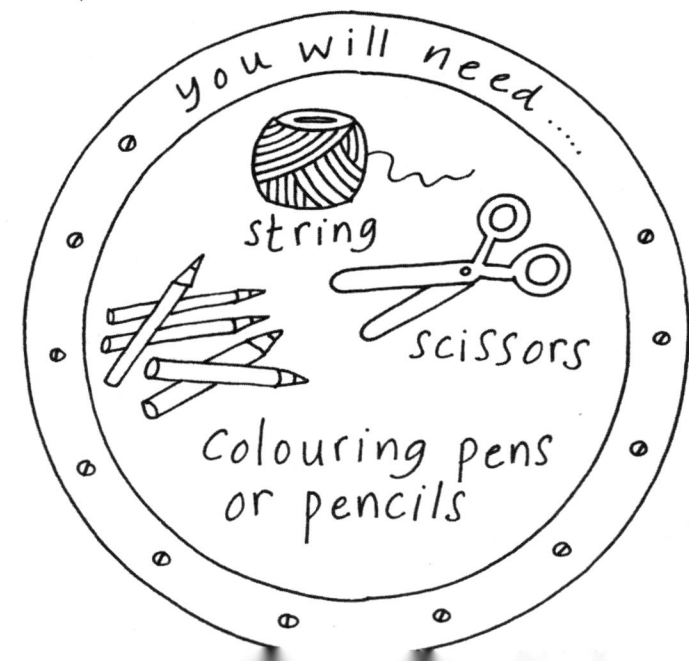

you will need....
- string
- scissors
- colouring pens or pencils

① Colour in the mask in bright scary colours.

② Cut out carefully and thread string through each side.

③ Then practise making monster noises and scare your friends!

If you don't want to spoil your book, why don't you trace the shape of the mask onto a cereal packet and make up your own scary design!

Millie's Marine Mosaics

Sailors have always recorded their most exciting adventures in paintings, stories and sometimes mosaics. Make your own mosaics of beautiful colourful fish.

You will need...
- scissors
- magazines or coloured paper
- glue

① Cut small squares from bright magazine pages or coloured paper.

② Carefully stick the squares onto the fish. The tail, fins and head might need smaller squares.

③ You could cut out your mosaic and pin it on the wall or turn it into a card for a friend or make a mobile.

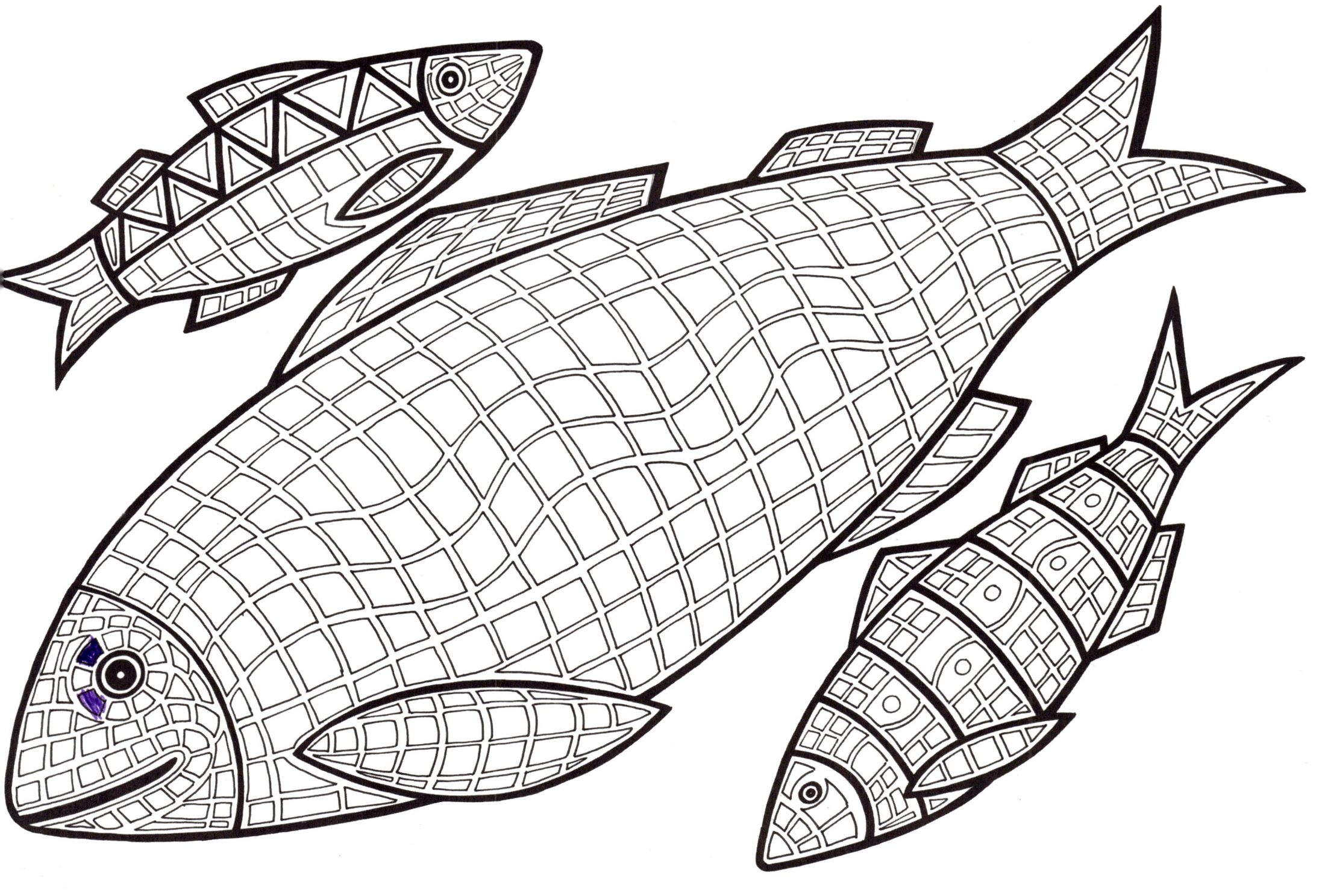

Pirate Pete's hat & Medal

You can tell an important sailor by the number of medals he wears. Try making this medal that Pete stole from a very angry admiral! Pirates often wore hats marked with the skull and crossbones to frighten their victims - try Pete's hat on for size.

Medal

① Glue the strips of ribbon or cloth on top of each other to make vertical stripes.

② Then cut out two circles of card and two circles of foil (try drawing around an egg cup for a good size) stick one circle of foil to each circle of card.

③ Use a blunt pencil to press shapes and patterns into the card. This will make an embossed effect on the foil side. Stick one circle to one side of your material and the other to the opposite side.

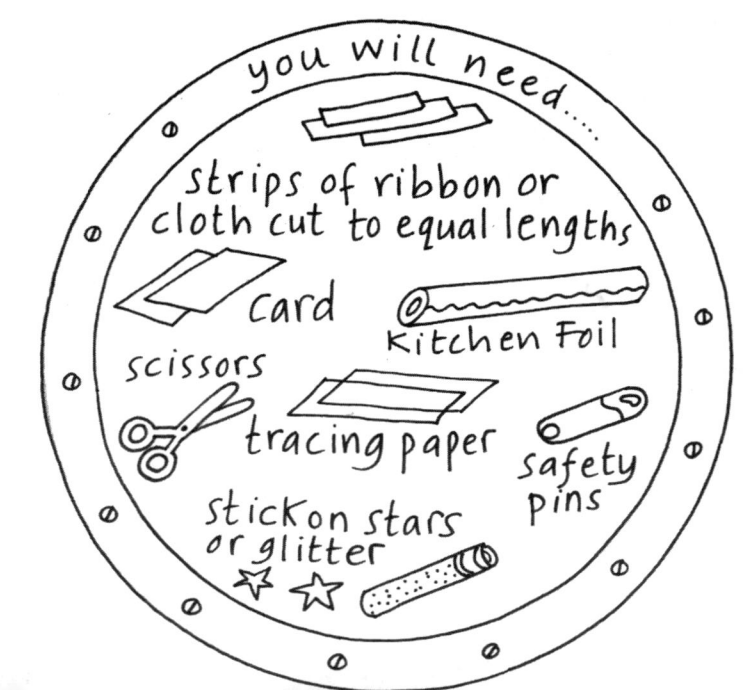

you will need....
- strips of ribbon or cloth cut to equal lengths
- card
- kitchen foil
- scissors
- tracing paper
- safety pins
- stick on stars or glitter

Millie's Mermaid Mirror

Mermaids are mythical creatures. In ancient stories and fairy tales beautiful mermaids would lure sailors to dangerous rocky shores with their hypnotic voices. If you have ever been on a cross channel ferry you will know that looking beautiful at sea is not easy! All mermaids and mermen need a mirror and a comb to keep a check on their appearance.

1. Trace and cut out the mirror shape from card and paint one side in a dark colour.
2. Turn over and cover the other side with brightly coloured cut out fish and starfish shapes.
3. Decorate with sequins, glitter and small pieces of foil.
4. Cut out a circle of foil and stick onto the dark undecorated side.
5. Trace and cut out the comb shape and paint and decorate as before. Then sit back and admire yourself!

you will need... card, paint, silver foil, glue, sequins and glitter

Sam Snorkel at the beach!

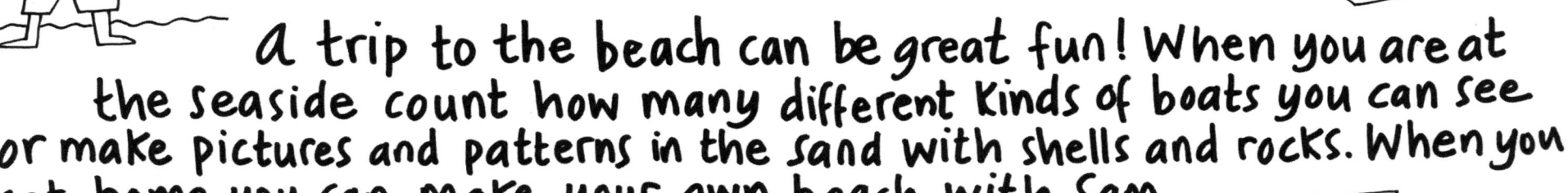

A trip to the beach can be great fun! When you are at the seaside count how many different kinds of boats you can see or make pictures and patterns in the sand with shells and rocks. When you get home you can make your own beach with Sam.

you will need...
- scissors
- card
- glue
- tracing paper
- colouring pens and pencils

① Fold a sheet of card in half to make an 'L' shape.

② Colour in one half of the card as a sunny sky and one half as the sand. — sky / sand

③ Then trace or cut out the shapes opposite. Colour them in and glue onto your beach scene using the small tabs.
(Colour in the tabs the colour of the sand so that they won't show.

④ Try drawing your own drawings or make different scenes of your friends on holiday using photographs.

All at Sea!

See you soon!

goodbye!

Education and interpretation at the National Maritime Museum

The Museum's Education and Interpretation Group provide a full and varied programme of events and resources for schools and the general public.

To obtain a copy of our latest Events leaflet contact:
0208 312 6649

For further details of our programmes for schools contact:
0208 312 6642

Written by Jane Ace & Alasdair Macleod
With additional ideas from:
Laura Bedford, Rachel Benton, Stuart Frost, Val Garwood & Stuart Slade
Designed & Illustrated by Liberation Design Consultants, Greenwich
All text and illustrations © National Maritime Museum, London, 2000
www.nmm.ac.uk
National Maritime Museum Website

We hope you enjoyed this book!

bye!

Don't forget to be careful near water!